Tales of
Fish, Boats & the Sea

⚓

And Other Fun Stuff

Captain Jeff Waxman

ISBN 978-1-62806-322-6   (print | paperback)

Library of Congress Control Number 2021911861

Published by Salt Water Media
29 Broad Street, Suite 104
Berlin, MD 21811
www.saltwatermedia.com

Salt-Water
MEDIA

Cover image courtesy of Joe Perez; interior images provided by the author
Cover design by Salt Water Media
Editing by Bill Cecil

TALES OF
FISH, BOATS & THE SEA

Dedicated to Eileen, my rock!

Table of Contents

Author's Note

Simply stated, my entire adult life has been focused on business interests intertwined with fishing (plus a hunting trip or two). And, with a decent tail wind, tons of good fortune and more hardworking than I'll admit to; I have managed to do pretty well in both. I have been CEO of five software companies, owned lots of boats, fished with some of the very best in the business, caught more than my share of fish ... but most of all, have had great fun.

But of far greater importance, I've tried to be a good husband to Eileen, and a good dad to my two daughters: Jaime and Jessi. Made more than my share of mistakes indeed but have always done my best. In retrospect, no regrets. God bless and Godspeed to all my friends and foes alike! Hope you enjoy "Book Two."

- Jeff Waxman

Chapter 1:
Swordfish Savant

⚓

If you've ever taken up daytime swordfishing,
one of the guys to thank for the fishery is Nick Stanczyk!

It started back in mid-December 2017. I had been writing a column called "Old Salts Rule!" for the professionals' sport-fishing magazine *InTheBite* and was asked to write about one of the charter guys running out of Bud N' Mary's Marina in Islamorada, Florida. Usually, I did the interviews by phone, but since we winter in the Keys, figured might be fun to drive up and meet face to face for a bit.

So, got there a bit early, seemed to be a slow day so hung around the store for a bit. Another old guy and I started to chat and quickly realized we knew tons of the same folks, had fished lots of the same places; we hit it off pretty good. After an hour or maybe two, we introduced ourselves and I met Richard Stanczyk, owner of Bud N' Mary's, and father to two super successful charter captains, Rick and Nick. Rick generally fished backcountry whilst Nick has made a name as one of the "founders" of daytime swordfishing. Our conversation was engrossing as Richard was clearly a man who had some of the most and best experiences in the game.

By this time, I had pretty much forgotten my plan for the day and we continued to talk over coffee. Proud father asked then if I had done any daytime swording, to which the answer was no, after which he suggested that I ride out with Nick for a day. Now, I doubted that Nick wanted someone to ride with him, but Richard was insistent and said to text Nick the next day. Well, I did so and to my surprise Nick texted back, laughingly worried that his dad had a habit of long conversations, (which Richard did and I do as well ... lol). So, Nick offered an invitation to join him in January on a day when he was fishing just one angler, which I graciously accepted immediately.

Early the morning planned, I arrived and watched Nick and his mate rig weights for the day (#11 rebar with taped on drop off hooks for hand cranking on hookup). The sole angler shows up, Mark Davis—one of the world's best who already had 15 or more Royal Slams to his credit. Easy going, thoughtful, and just plain nice guy, Mark was a gentleman and had just received an award from IGFA a day or two before for heavyweight angling success for the prior year! And then, while we were doing the "get to know each other" chat, we had an interesting bit of crossover. In the current month's *InTheBite* magazine, there was a long exceptional article about Mark and his Rybovich in Hawaii, written by an associate, Ric Burnley. And—the very next article? A story written by yours truly: a three-page "Old Salts Rule!" column about Bouncer Smith. What a way to start a great day!

Soon as the light allowed, off we headed: Mark in the cock-

Mark and mate with pomfret

pit lying down, the mate getting the boat ready, Nick beside me finishing a bowl of cereal, and me happily watching and learning. The day clear, wind brisk (for me, very brisk) but the Freeman 37 ate up the chop. We ran a bit over an hour out to the first drop of the day, 1800 feet to start the drift. Watching the drop and drift set up was intriguing, having not done so before—it was very orchestrated and formulaic—easy to explain, not so easy to do.

First drift, bait down, Mark at the ready; seas choppy but the Freeman drifted perfectly. Ten minutes and slightest dip of the rod tip—hooked up! Mark began to hand crank, long way up. The fish fought, but (to me) unexpectedly light. As we saw color,

Mate with pomfret

we understood why: the first fish was a beautiful 25-ish pound Pomfret! Black body, silvery scimitar of a tail—and great eating.

Drift number two: seas build a bit, back to start point, drop 'n' drift. Ten more minutes, slightest dip, hooked up! And again, Mark hand cranked, this time though, the fight was as expected, and after maybe 15 or 20 minutes on a 50, our first sword of the day come into view: approximately 90 to 100 lb. of beautiful silver flanks, huge broad eye, and very angry. Nick released him quickly, the mate picked another bait, and we swung back into the current once again.

Drop three ... and four ... and five and six ... each drop followed suit. Nick was proving his skills beyond comparison. At each drop, we hooked up and Mark hand cranked a sword to the

First sword release

Second sword release

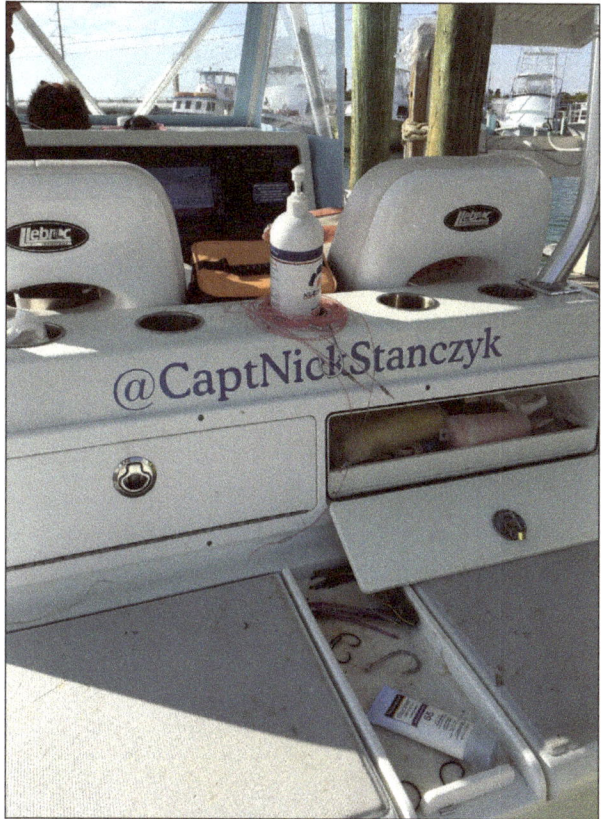

Tackle cabinet on 37-foot Freeman

surface. The fish were all in the 90- to 150-lb. range, each one a beautiful healthy sword, each one released. The seas were building a bit, the Freeman still comfortable, but a few waves tossed spray up and over the gunwales. For me, it was getting rough.

By mid-afternoon, Nick had proven to me to be a Swordfish Savant—no doubt, no comparison. We had a Pomfret in the box, five swords hooked and released. It was now two-thirty in the afternoon. Nick asked about another drop. Mark laughed and said, "Head for the barn, we've had a great day." Well, I was glad to head back for sure, I had the company of a truly great fisherman, a world-class captain and a quiet but hugely skillful mate.

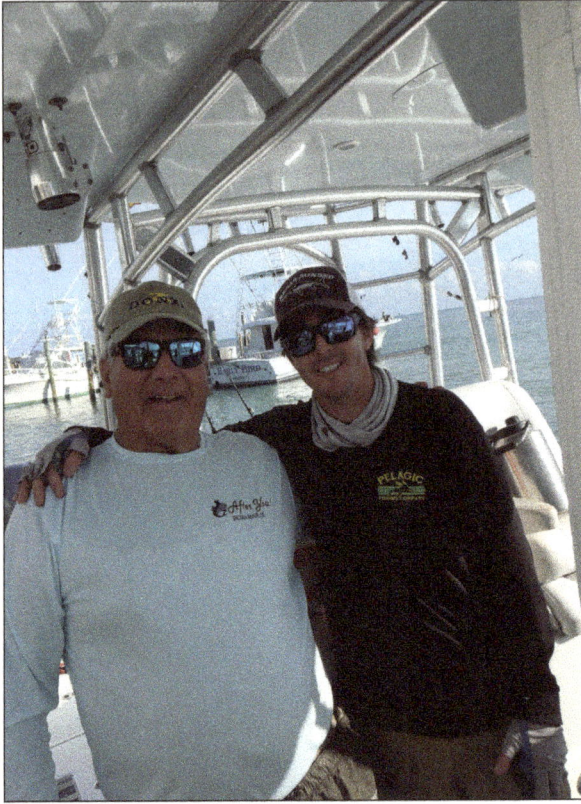

Author and Nick

The ride in was wet, a bit bumpy, but not bad given the skillful boat handling. We hit the fuel dock by three-thirty, Mark jumped off and headed for dinner; Nick fueled up and was at the slip by just past four. Nick and the mate had the boat cleaned and ready for next day trip within half an hour.

What a day! Met wonderful folks, learned a ton about a new fishery from the best. Richard and Nick, I thank you both greatly for the hospitality. Bud N' Mary's really is the "Sportfishing Capital of the World". Think about this for a moment: six drops, six fish! Mark hand cranked over a mile of line. What a trip.

Chapter 2:
Tuff To Admit, But ...

⚓

If catching a blue marlin in the wrong canyon isn't embarrassing enough, this one goes to the head of the class. Put this in the "How the hell did you do that" category.

October 15, 2020, trying to salvage a decent fishing year out a very lousy season. Swordfishing getting good, several boats hooking up, we plan a trip on Dr. Pat's *Priceless*, a 31-foot Bertram. The swordfish crew consisted of two top guys, Steve and Nolan, plus a friend of Steve's, Doc, and me. Doc runs the boat, occasionally I'll help out on a deep drift, but we were set. The plan was to pull out at five, so I set the clock for 4:00 a.m.

Mid-evening, I get a text from my friend Dan, captain of 62-foot Viking *SeaFlame* (with SeaKeeper, important to note). The *Flame* was gonna stop at the 30 Fathom Lump for a quick shot at tuna, then off to the deep for swordie drift. And to be sure, this was an embarrassment of riches in my mind. I was committed already, but an invite on the *Flame* was always an honor. We agreed to stay in contact through the day; it was gonna be good!

The radio was set, clothes laid out, lunch and drinks in the fridge, bed came early, asleep by maybe 11 ish. Woke with a start, something didn't seem right, grabbed the phone wherein the clock was set ... it was 5:20 a.m. WTF! Even amidst the brain fog, it was obviously late—very, very late. Quickly called Doc to say, "Go without me." They'd been waiting and wondering since I'm usually early. Quickly thought, "*Flame* leaving at five-thirty, can I make it? Nope, not a shot." Completely befuddled, got up, turned on coffee and realized I had somehow managed to set for p.m., not a.m. It seems that when we changed the "leave-the-dock" time and I reset the clock (phone really), I hit p.m. Duh!

So, here I was ... all dressed up and nowhere to go. My buddies were fishing, I was on dry land; truly felt like an idiot. Only sensible plan, be at the dock early, meet the boys and dodge the well-earned certain abuse to come.

Got to the marina by maybe 4:30 p.m., the *Flame* came in shortly thereafter. They had a helluva day! Got to the Lump to take a crack at tuna and never left: tuna were thick—they hit plugs, they hit live bait, they hit ballyhoo. Ten tuna in the box, all on light tackle and all weighing from 63 to 75 lb. Over 600 lb. of tuna on the hoof! Dan had done it, put the boys right on them. Justin and Jimmy were the team of mates, and the anglers clicked. They hit it perfectly.

Meanwhile, given mid-October timing, the weather had shifted; it started to blow (hard) and sunset was early. Doc was slogging through a messy sea on the way home. The *Flame* crew had the boat cleaned, the fish cleaned (300-plus lb. of fresh yellowfin) bagged up and getting ready to leave; it was dusk when Doc pulled in. They had quite a ride home: wet, bumpy, slower than the usual 25 knots, but the 31-footer was a tank, the en-

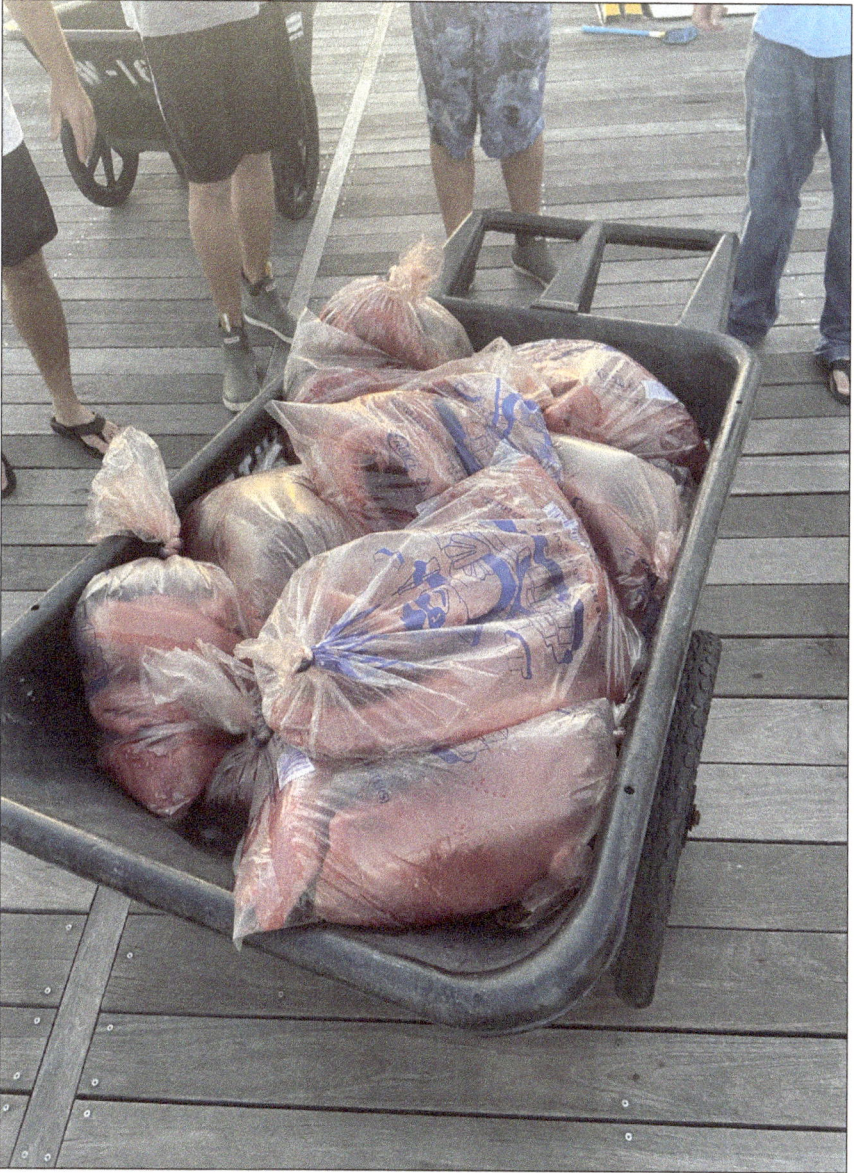

300 lb. of fresh caught yellowfin tuna!

Author with 5 lb. of fresh tuna sashimi...
with extra virgin olive oil, capers, and lemon juice!

First sword
caught on *Priceless*
105 lb.
Wilmington Canyon

closure was rock solid, and they were relaxed, drinking a Bloody Mary and taking their time. They too had a good day!

Once set up, they had managed four long drifts from shallow to deep. Starting at 1200 feet, they fished one deep line, no buoy line. Doc handled the boat like a pro, keeping the line mostly vertical regardless of the changing currents in the deep canyon edges. They caught one 105 lb. sword on drift two. No bites on drifts one and three. The seas were building but on drift four, the rod tip didn't just dip once or twice, it loaded up and slammed down, hard, fully bent into a horseshoe! And stayed loaded for minutes with the fish taking line—and then, it went slack. Bait destroyed, line showing fray above the bait, but *no bueno* ... gone. Time for the barn. Seventy-five miles back from the Wilmington

Swordfish loin being steaked out!

canyon to the dock in freshening winds and building seas. Just take your time, take what the ocean gives you, don't push it and get home safely.

And so, as the result of cockpit error on my part, I managed to miss not one but two damn fine fishing days. Yet, my buddies were truly kind; I left for home that evening with three nice swordie steaks (thanks to Doc and the boys) and a bag of two huge tuna loins (thanks to Dan and the boys). Screwup in timing notwithstanding, I feel truly honored to be blessed with such good friends!

Shoutout to Doc, Steve, Nolan, Dan, Andrew, Justin, Jimmy ... thank you. From the guy who can't tell time!

CHAPTER 3:
LAST DAY OF OCTOBER 2020 ...
WE NEED A GOOD ENDING TO 2020
DEEP DROP TRIP

As we all know 2020 was a difficult year at best. COVID affected everything and everyone, masks were required, and social distancing was the order of the day. Tournaments were affected, travel was affected, and so many people lost businesses—some lost lives. It was not a good year. My good friend, Capt. Joe Perez, boat- and hunting-property partner, passed unexpectedly in July. Not much good about 2020. He is much missed!

We usually fish the White Marlin Open in early August on Dr. Pat's 31-foot Bertram *Priceless*. But our crew from Long Island was quarantined and the service for Joe was that week, so I was out. The tourney, for us, was a bust. We tried to make a silk purse out of a day or two fishing after the tourney and ran offshore on a makeup trip the Tuesday afterward. We added insult to injury. Not only did we catch nothing of note, but 12 miles offshore we hit a deadhead at 25 knots and bent both rudders—

Dave and Doc with first tile of the day

Dave with blueline tile—a full pound over the world's record!

badly! We were lucky not to have torn the starboard rudder out of its housing. It was a bad hit on a submerged object. We were lucky, we limped in, got pulled and sat on the hard. As usual, the insurance folks and the repair folks did their best, but we still sat for six weeks until all was well, passed the sea trial and ready to go. It was early October, nearing the end of fishing, as hunting was coming into focus.

So, we did a preliminary run, testing the systems on a fun run with two friends, mates on a local headboat. We had a couple sets of deep drop numbers in the Poor Man's canyon and gave them a try; it's 2020—nothing! We tried several numbers we had been given more nothing. It was getting late and October sun sets early, so we ran to our old standby numbers in the Baltimore. After several drifts, we had picked up a handful of tilefish, one maybe 15 lb., the rest 5 to 7 lb. We boxed about 70 lb., but it was late, and we were 65 miles to the sea buoy. We ran 25 knots; sunset was in an hour. Heading home in the dark. For the first time Doc was inlet-running using track lines and range lights. And it went flawlessly. Boat handling and inlet-running were superb, the fish-cleaning crew stayed open for us. It was a decent day, but still just not the day to end the season.

The weather sucked, wind and rain most every day. Black powder deer season came and went, wet, windy, and warm; not hunting weather, not fishing weather. It began to look as if our fishing year would end—not on our hoped-for good, solid day— but rather on a just-okay day. Could be worse.

During the last few days, I drove to NC to pick up a few things from my buddy's home to help his widow, more just to be there than really do anything. Got home late on the afternoon

Author with only small fish—about 10 lb.

of the next to last day of the month, and hour or so later, Dr. Pat called. "Good forecast, let's go tomorrow!". Sure sounded good, although we were pretty unprepared. We decided to leave a bit later than usual (*Priceless* typically left before dawn, but we decided to leave at 7:30 instead) and run directly to our best numbers. It was a make-or-break trip, trying to end a mediocre-at-best year on a good note. The plan was set!

We scrounged a package of cobia belly for bait—best tilefish bait ever—tough and hugely attractive. We brought our deep jig rods with 850-gram jigs with single hooks on either end. And to be safe, brought two electric assists in case we needed to explore if fish were not exactly on our numbers. (We use electrics to explore rather than hand-crank jigs once we find the fish). And, since the crew was only the two of us, I invited the captain of a local private boat, Dave Long, to join us.

We arrived at our numbers at 10:30 a.m.—clear skies, no breeze, cobalt-blue ocean. It looked perfect. And it was, except for two things (the devil is in the details): 1) fish were not there, and 2) current was running—hard! But, after a short drift, maybe 150 feet away, we found a tiny "covey" of fish. Doc had one on the deck, roughly 20 lb., a trophy-sized blueline. And so, we made our usual adjustments—Doc and Dave in the cockpit, yours truly at the helm, and we made the exact same drift each time. We hooked one, and occasionally two, per drift. The fish were in a very tight group; we could only hook up in the exact spot on each pass, and given the ripping current at about 2.5 knots, we could not get bottom in 400 feet with jigs, so stayed with the electric assists.

And, what a day's catch! We caught our limit—nine blueline

Doc with final fish—22 lb.

tiles—all from 19 to 23 lb.—unheard of! All in the exact same drift, all within 10 to 20 yards of each other. And one more anomaly: a gator-sized bluefish on the bottom at 400 feet. Go figure. Our largest fish was almost a pound OVER the state record but did not qualify, being caught on electric assist Daiwa 800 MJ.

By two o'clock, we picked up for the barn. It was 50 degrees when we left, maybe 75 in the Canyon and back down to 50-ish when reaching the dock. Flat calm run home, washed down on the run, and made the fish cleaner by 4:30 p.m. with half an hour to spare.

In our own small way, we had ended our very difficult fishing year on the note we had hoped for: a good trip, a good catch, and a nice day, with good memories to carry us into the year to come. Doc, Dave, and I really needed a good one, and we greatly appreciated our good fortune and thanked the fish and weather gods.

Chapter 4:
Booby Bait Boat

⚓

Oregon Inlet, NC, June 1981. After ten years at offshore fishing, we had become completely focused on Oregon Inlet fishing, and we were hooked! The fishing was as good as it gets on the East Coast, the run was close in (30 to 35 miles typically), and the charter boats freely shared information, looking out for us private rigs. Unless you were a local charter, you were referred to as an "outboard," regardless of size or skill. Flags were flown only for billfish—all released—and it was a great place to learn the offshore game.

By this time, I had acquired a beach house in Nags Head, had partnered with my buddy Joe on a 36-foot private rig, a custom-built Harris gas boat, fully equipped, complete with bridge and fighting chair. I was working as an executive in a multinational corporation and managed to fish every weekend the weather allowed, usually with Joe at the helm and me in the cockpit. And had begun to seriously date a woman who seemed to want to share the fishing experience. Life was good.

Occasionally though, Joe would not make a weekend. He

owned and was president of a computer service company—a bit more responsibility than yours truly. And so, on this weekend, the crew was girlfriend and me. Now, girlfriend had dived headfirst into fishing, she wanted to catch everything, learned to rig baits, and even bought a mate's pliers of her very own. She had caught a few fish and was doing pretty well, even by Oregon Inlet terms. And, she had become friends with several of the other mates and captains, trying hard to fit in!

And so, on this weekend, with a crew of two, we decided to start the day slowly. Breakfast at Sam & Omie's restaurant, rig baits at the dock, and head off to the Point at about 7:45. I was on the bridge at the helm, the plan was to make it easy and fish four lines out of the cockpit, girlfriend had the pit to herself. The sea was flat, the sun was hot, and the fleet was over the hundred picking up yellowfins and dolphin. The radio was buzzing, and I was looking forward to a nice easy run.

Given our short-handed crew, I figured we would set up three or four miles inshore of the main fleet and be prepared once we got into the fish. And, truth be known, I didn't really have high confidence in my mate. So, we set up four cockpit lines, all sea witch ballyhoos (it was 1981) and three minutes later, a white one hooked up! Girlfriend fought the fish well; we managed to fight and release without any problems. I got the three lines in, she fought the fish, billed and released it, way inshore of the fleet in 30 fathoms of green water. And during the fight, I saw several other whites working the same area! Clearly not expected.

So, we set up again. Girlfriend was hot from the fight, the sun was hot, so girlfriend took off her shirt—she had a great figure—was topless, but nobody was around so she felt comfortable.

And then, left long rigger went off—blue marlin! Hooked up, smallish fish, but tearing up the surface. Given the second billfish in minutes, I called the fleet in to my numbers (LORAN at the time). And they came, the entire fleet of maybe twenty or more boats, all heading our way.

Meanwhile, girlfriend very topless in the chair fighting her fish. And over the next hour or so, most every boat came by—close by—to offer encouragement, and of course, take her picture! She called me words that would have caused a sailor to blush; perhaps my laughter was under appreciated? But whatever reason, while calling me everything but decent, we did manage a release on a 300-pound-ish blue one. I thought it was great day! After the release and an hour of a sulking mate, we caught a small yellowfin and headed for the barn.

Now, in retrospect, it appears that she just didn't enjoy the rest of the season like Joe and I did. We were nicknamed for a while, the "Boat with the Booby Mate" and the endless discussion of the "special bait" we used was great fun—for us. Joe and I at least!

CHAPTER 5:
A WAY WITH WORDS—SOMETIMES GOOD OLE BOYS SAY THINGS PERFECTLY!

⚓

Mid-summer, 1978—we were fishing a marlin tournament out of Destin, Florida, in the Panhandle. The crew was just three of us, all working for Xerox amidst its heyday, in John Ogletree's brand new 38-foot Bertram, *Bottom Line*. I had been invited to work the pit; our angler was Mike Long. Both John and Mike were old friends from Alabama. And although both had successful careers in business, when together they slipped quickly into the vernacular speech of the South. John was "Jawwhnn" and Mike was "Maahhck"—both Southernized and elongated into three full syllables!

The tournament was slow, we had one first-day release but nothing since; we were late in day three, the last day, and very much not in the hunt. Seas were flat, we trolled at seven knots to cover more water such that the 3126 Cats droned us into boredom and almost hypnosis on the bridge where the three of us sat. At maybe two-ish, John sorta woke up and asked Mike for a bit of lunch: "Maybe a sandwich, please?" Mike sorta stared back and climbed down and into the salon. And a few minutes later, came into the cockpit and the following sleepy conversation occurred.

Mike: "Jaawwhhnn, if we had some cheese, you could have a ham and cheese, if we had some ham." After maybe thirty seconds, John responded: "Thank you, Maaahhhcck, that sounds good," in a very slow drawl. Mike then climbed back up the ladder, assumed his spot and we finished the day, trolling with no bites.

To me, the interchange was flawless, a perfect response that to this day brings a smile. Gotta love the Good Ole Boys at their best!

CHAPTER 6:
FIRST OFFSHORE TRIP
FIRST BLUE MARLIN—UNCUT HEROIN!

⚓

As we all know 2020 was a difficult year at best. COVID affected everything and everyone, masks were required, and social distancing was the order of the day. Tournaments were affected, travel was affected, and so many people lost businesses—some lost lives. It was not a good year. My good friend, Capt. Joe Perez, boat- and hunting-property partner, passed unexpectedly in July. Not much good about 2020.

Summer 1973, if memory serves, and this is how it all began. I had just been promoted from sales into my first management job. My new boss, Chris by name, was an accomplished marlin fisherman, half owner of a 31-foot Bertram running out of Ocean City, the *El Tigre*. His partner, Paul, was also an accomplished offshore guy, although in retrospect, the boat was gas powered, a floating junk pile, and Capt. Bud (for Budweiser) lived on it! But they caught fish and Chris regaled me with stories of greyhounding billfish and back-breaking tuna.

My fishing had been successful, but limited to bluefish, flounder, striped bass—and I once even caught a bonito in the chum slick. I was enthralled by the stories. And so, late that summer, they invited me to be the third member of the crew to fish two days out of Hatteras! Truth be known, I nonchalantly said yes, but inside was more excited than a nine-year-old expecting a Red Ryder BB gun. I mildly suspected that my presence was to help cover costs, but it mattered not. A weekend big game fishing off "Hatras" was a very big deal.

Now it helps to realize that both these guys were world-class reprobates in many ways: drinking way too much, womanizing with the best of them, and cutting corners at every turn. So, a few days before heading out, Chris told me they were bringing a woman "friend" and suggested that I might oughta do the same. Fitting neatly into the same description (painfully honesty here), I too had a "friend." She worked in the same office and was a secretary to one of the managers who worked for Chris. Samantha very much wanted to come, so off we went in a borrowed station wagon, way before SUVs existed, but pretty similar. My only surprise was that my buddies had one "friend" between them. Oh well, we were going to "Hatras" to marlin fish.

The drive down was uneventful, assuming drinking endless beers, getting lost twice, and stopping every hundred miles to empty our bladders qualifies as such. Dinner was 7-11 hot dogs on Route 12 well after midnight, although they had been on the rollers since morning. But the good news, we did not need rooms as we arrived at Oden's Dock maybe 4:00 a.m. just as the mate also arrived. The boat was the *Early Bird*, captained by Emory Dillon, quite well respected indeed. Our mate, a young guy named Chip Shafer, who over the years became one of the most respected captains in the game, running his boat *Temptress* and winning tournaments up and down the coast.

And after the semi-drunken, very sleepy introductions, off we went through "Hatras" Inlet to the Gulf Stream. I was entranced and wide awake as the aptly named *Early Bird* left early and got there late. We maybe cruised at 14 knots, maybe, or even less, but the run was about 24 to 25 miles and we started to fish. Finally, the outriggers made sense to a true novice. The fighting chair made sense; it even had a canvas harness draped over it. And, to my total and complete surprise, you could actually SEE YOUR BAITS. I was over the moon!

Marlin fishing, for real. If memory serves, we had six baits out, five sea witched ballyhoo, and a flapping Spanish on the long right. Hard as I watched the baits, I only saw the ballyhoo when they skipped; the Spanish was easier to see. About mid-morning, my "crew" awoke, the guys coming to the cockpit drinking coffee and the girls off to the bow in various stages of cover. Although the guys were focused on fishing, somehow the captain and mate seemed more interested in the show on the bow. One of the girls even managed to sunburn both ass cheeks, which made for great fun later at her expense.

Once awake and semi-functional, Chris assigned rods to each of us; left long and short were mine for starters, although they were barely visible to my untrained eye. Right long and short were Paul's, and Chris had the two flat lines. It was mesmerizing; watching and waiting, hot sun, drone of the engines, half-naked women on the bow.

And then, in a shout, "There he is!" Huge splash hit the Spanish, Paul freespooled the 80, and after what seemed like minutes, thumbed the drag to strike—and it was on! The first real live blue marlin I had ever seen was greyhounding off the starboard transom. He ran, jumped, ran, jumped, then sounded. After maybe an hour, a smallish blue one, maybe 200 lb., was tired and near the end of the fight. Chip wanted to assure a safe release, so he gloved up and grabbed hold on the bill on the port side, Emory keeping the boat moving forward to get water through the fish's gills. And then, Chip appeared to be jumping up and down, maybe a foot or more each jump, when the fish came to life and tossed him around like a dishrag. Emory came screaming off the bridge, cut the leader and the fish was free, jumped once, and was gone. Emory had "words" with his mate. All I remember is "green fish" which made no sense at the time given the marlin was blue. But I learned afterward what it all meant.

Heaven. Blue marlin fought and released—the stuff of dreams. Two dolphins, no other bites, and back to the dock where we learned that the next day, instead of fishing "Hatras," our boat (the Mel-O-Dee captained by Buddy Cannaday) had run back north to Oregon Inlet where fishing had picked up. Quick dinner at the Red Drum and off to Oregon Inlet where Chris had found our ragtag crew one room with two queen beds. No matter, we were exhausted and due at the dock at 5:00 a.m.

The next day was eventful although nowhere near as exciting. We caught a box of "dawlphin" (in the captain's Elizabethan dialect) and I caught a white marlin and learned the difference between white and blue in real time. The girls seemed to be in another world, even though the single engine boat was only 34-foot long. Our mate, Billy McAskill, ended up owning *Whalebone Tackle*, and our captain "BC" became well known for his custom boats.

And so, it began—I was hooked—like heroin straight into the vein. Changed my life for sure and lord knows the amount of time and money spent as the result of that first trip.

Chapter 7:
Every Boat is a Compromise!

⚓

The more you learn about boats, the more you realize that every boat is a compromise. There are big and small boats, flats boats and bay boats, deep vee and flat bottom boats, and on and on. Now, to be sure, unless your choice of fishing is tightly specific and you choose a specific boat, you'll spend somewhere around $6 million before you get awfully close to perfection, at least for the offshore crowd. Oh, and do remember to add in a full-time captain, assume approximately $5,000 per offshore trip, but you will get pretty close.

Nonetheless, for most of us, compromise is required. In my case, having gotten married and moved from the Outer Banks of NC (where the run was roughly 30 to 35 miles and the fishing world class) to Indian River, Delaware, a compromise was required. I owned and ran a Buddy Davis 47-footer, hull number one, charter boat finished for sure, but great sea boat. We cruised in low 20s, burned maybe 40 gph, and had the normal issues, wear and tear, and hour-plus long clean-up per trip. But the run was now doubled each way, making for considerable fuel burn

Best Revenge coming in from The Point on a sporty day, with limit of yellowfins in the box. We ran a single engine 8 v92Ti cruised comfortably at 20-21 knots. Juniper hull, glassed over, charter boat finished. Burned about 120-130 gallons per day, full keel, blacked out windows were solid. Huge cockpit and salon, tackle cabinets on either side of salon doors, companionway bunks and stateroom (sorta) forward. Good boat in its day!

and very long days. Plus, approaching retirement age, handling the boat without a dedicated crew was becoming undoable—just too much fuel, time, and energy. I was now married, living in Delaware, and in need of a very different rig. Plus—I was "old"!

And so began the process of deciding what would be the baseline requirement to handle this new fishery, complete with multiple competitive needs. The checklist covered for me:

Buddy Davis Hull #1, my charter boat at Oregon Inlet Fishing Center in early 1980s. Bull Tolson was first Captain, I filled in at times. We did well. Boat was the *Best Revenge*.

1) Range: minimum of 300 miles with reserve;

2) Center Console: 30 to 35 feet. Able to handle redundant electronics in dash;

3) Hull: only deep vee considered. Handle moderate seas comfortably;

4) Storage: for tackle, inboard fish boxes, ice, bait, tackle cabinet;

5) Speed: 30 to 35 knot cruise and reasonably efficient;

6) Name brand / cost / value: no need to add 10 to 20% for certain brand names.

Stern shot of *Best Revenge*.
Captain Bull on the bridge setting out the spread!

Given the list above, the options narrowed quickly. February 2006: went to Miami Boat Show with four or five boats in mind. After two days of looking, comparing, kicking tires, etc., made a decision and ordered my new—and likely last—boat. Ordered directly through the president of the company and agreed to pay local dealer full normal commission in order for them to handle delivery and set-up plus any future issues. (Note: after 16 years of usage, still happy with that decision). May 2006, new Donzi 35 ZFC delivered to me at Indian River Marina. Z for hull type, F for fishing configuration, and C for cuddy cabin just what I needed.

We run twin 300 Verados, carry over 300 gallons of fuel, and cruise comfortably at 35 knots. We burn a gallon per mile at

Donzi 35 ZFC *After You* at rest

speed—very efficient indeed, even to the point of forward reserve tank and pump to main in order to keep best balance, with huge K-plane trim tabs. If rough, we stay at the dock. Perfect for four head, ok for five; redundant top of line electronics, great for trolling or deep drops, good for flounder and sea bass as well.

Total of forty rod holders, including rocket launchers, gunwales, transom and bow rails, plus cuddy cabin storage for heavy tackle and light and in between—comfortably and safely! And, completely cleaned and done in 15 minutes. Are there things to change or modify? Surprisingly few, really. Main consideration was new power after six hard years of running, now on second set and completely pleased.

And so, where are we? Given that our marina is small and

Donzi 35 ZFC *After You* **on the water**

that most of the serious fishing folk know each other, lots of us fish together. Depending on who and how many, when we go and the weather helps decide which boat. Since I'm retired and pretty much around, happy to go with friends or take friends; it usually works well.

Advice? Given that it's worth what you pay for it, here is mine. Decide what you want to do with your boat, how many people you want to do it with, and what you can afford initially and operationally before you look. And don't be swayed by shiny objects!

CHAPTER 8:
IT'S ON THE MENU, OF COURSE!

⚓

Late July 1978, Oregon Inlet, NC. My partner, Joe Perez, and I had taken 10 days off, planning to fish every day. We stayed at my beach house and fished the *Reel Time*, Joe's custom 36-foot Harris. Most days we had a couple other buddies with us, weather was good, but fishing was sorta slow. A few whites had shown up, dolphin were schooled in weed lines, tuna pretty much gone for the time being.

After maybe four days of fishing, the phone rang around 10:00 p.m. It was the Oregon Inlet fishing center manager, and they needed help for the next day. Seems a yearly fishing group chartered 10 boats, paid for by their company, a coal mine in West Virginia. The miners looked forward to the trip yearly, but one boat was broken down, and we were asked to take the four-man crew. Of course, we agreed (we were insured as a charter and both of us had six-pack tickets) and met the party the next morning. They were standing behind the boat waiting when we arrived.

Three men and a boy, all in the exact outfits one would expect: blue coveralls, blue baseball caps, hard-soled shoes (with new sneakers in hand!) and jackets. We stifled a giggle, starting to ready the boat, when Joe asked, "What would you guys like to catch?"

I gave him a sideways glance and shook my head. The first man said in a slow drawl, "Well, I'd like to catch a marlin. The boss said he will pay for a mount." The second guy smiled and said, "Me, too!" The boy then added, "I wanna catch a shark!" And the last guy stood for a minute and then said, "Can I please catch a tuna fish, please, 'cause they taste really good!" My partner Joe answered, saying, "We'll do our best. No promises, but maybe so." I cut my eyes at him and just shook my head.

Sun starts to come up and we head out. Joe at the helm, yours truly in the pit. Our crew quiet but obviously very excited, watched every single move, every bait. We ran only single strand wire leaders then, 15-foot, usually #12 on ballyhoo and #15 on Spanish. On mullet we used #19 harder to twist but ran big baits better and tougher to kink. Had a box of baits rigged by the time we set out, got our guys situated, and had five ballyhoo in the spread, three skipping and two swimming. First hour nothing, then bam! Deep bait goes off on a blind strike with a whitey jumping off the transom! Fifteen minutes and he's in the boat, covered with towels and ice. We set up again.

Another hour goes by, a swirl and a bill shows behind a skipping bait, he takes it, turns to run; dropped back, set the hook—he's on! Whitey number two hooked up, fought on a 30 and within 20 minutes, he too is in the boat. I look up at Joe, he shrugs, grins, giggles, and cracks a beer. The rest of the nine boats chartered for the group pulled a total of three whites, couple of dolphins, couple empty. It's about noon. Joe decides to head overboard, nothing much going on. All of a sudden, Joe yells to me to, "Put out a Spanish and hold on to a 50." He sees a free-swimming mako, swings the Spanish in front him, slows down, then picks up speed. The mako slams the Spanish and we are hooked up immediately! Not a big mako, 120 lb., but what a fight; clears the water by 10 feet more than once. Finally, our boy gets the fish beside the boat (well, lotsa boat work), I gaff him, we tail rope him and drag him backwards until very surely dead. Our young boy was way too interested to take a chance!

It's around one-thirty with an hour of fishing time left; three fish in the cockpit, iced down under towels (no fish bags yet). I looked up at Joe with a big grin, when our last guy says, "Mr. Mate, I sure would like to catch me a tuna." Of course, they had no idea that we had caught exactly what they wanted, in exactly the order they asked! Pure, unadulterated luck on our part, and not one tuna caught in the fleet. Joe gave me a "hang on a second" finger shrug, got on the radio asking if anyone had ideas of where tuna might be found? Remember, it had been at least a week since the last tuna was brought in. Omie, on the *Sportsman*, came back in his slow deliberate way and said that he'd heard the longline guys maybe ten clicks to the north mention tuna pushing water, maybe give it a try. Quick thanks, we picked up and ran for half-hour straight up the line on the Hundred, then set out. Three lines out, getting ready to put out number four, and two lines go off!

One pulled the hook quickly and one ran, then settled down. We got our guy in the chair; he did the job and in 10 minutes gaffed a school-sized yellowfin and put him in the box. Time to head for the barn. Our crew was happy, pleased really, likely thinking that we had delivered "what they ordered." Joe and I sat on the bridge the whole ride in, giggling to ourselves about the day's events. How in the world had this really happened? We were beside ourselves, pleased for our crew of coal miners, pleased for our showing in the fleet, generally happy as hell. The 10 boats in the group all did well, we gained a touch of respect, and our first charter out of Oregon Inlet was a success.

The day ended on a poignant note. Our charter was paid for by the company, including food, mounts for billfish, fish cleaning, and even the sneakers they were each given to wear. But, as our crew left, each of the three men gave me a tip; each handed me a ten-dollar bill and said, "Thank you, Mr. Mate." With Joe's okay, just before they left, I called the boy over and gave him the leader and hook from his mako, then congratulated him and shook his hand, with the three ten-dollar bills bunched up in the handshake.

Ordered right off the menu!

And a final note of interest. Joe had retired by 1985. He bought and ran the charter boat *Fight-N-Lady* out of Oregon Inlet until 2018. Joe was my best buddy for forty years. We lost him in July 2020.

Chapter 9:
Boat Names

⚓

What could be more fun than choosing a name for your boat? Some folks have one name they use for every boat they own, some name each boat separately. Some are great, some good, some just ok, and some really suck. My only suggestion— think about how the name will: 1) wear over time, and 2) sound over the radio. Worst ever (in my humble opinion) was the name *Mmmm* on a really ugly, huge cruiser docked in a transient slip. I think it was perhaps a Carver.

So, with the above as a backdrop and since the question was asked, here goes. Opening myself to rampant comment, criticism, and perhaps worse—my boat names over the years:

> 1. *After You*: current 35-foot center console. After ordered, my two adult daughters each called separately (I'm certain they were in cahoots) and asked if I would name the boat after them. On the day of delivery, I called each girl and said, "Honey, I named the boat After You." The old man wasn't born yesterday.

2. *Best Revenge*: 47-foot Buddy Davis. Had just gone through a tough time and named the boat after the proverb "Living Well is the Best Revenge." And it was.

3. *Foxy Lady*: 30-foot Chris Craft Tournament Fisherman. Ray Hunt design, deep vee, great vest pocket Sportfish. Named after the Jimi Hendrix song.

Others included *Sun Chaser*, *Plan B*, *Long Shot*, plus many more which memory thankfully resists!

And, if you should have the chance, ask Eileen the story of the "marina contract and the boat name." It's her story and it's a gem!

CHAPTER 10:
FISHING IN THE LOWER KEYS—
A NEW WORLD!

⚓

We used to go to the British Virgins every winter, rent a 44-foot power cat, and spend 3 to 4 weeks wandering, fishing, drinking, and enjoying the postcard views in every direction. We had approval to pretty much cover from Anegada to St Maarten, carried fishing tackle, and had wonderful trips. And then, our dog sitter bought a condo in ski country, and we wouldn't leave our dog in a kennel, so change of plans.

Off to the Lower Florida Keys—Cudjoe Key to be exact—where it turns out several folks from our Delaware Marina winter. And so, we began to fish in new ways, even to the point of buying a book to identify the various fish caught! On many days, a four-hour trip would yield as many as 15 or more species! Ever heard of a squirrel fish? A beautiful orange little guy with ultra-sharply pointed gill plates to hold it in the reef crevasses—oh, and poison-tipped as well! Or figured out what to do with a four-foot green moray that seems to twist up the leader, with open mouth full of very sharp inward-pointed teeth? Yep, different indeed!

Yellowtails

Fishing the Keys in your own rig seems to fall into several buckets: trolling offshore for mahi or wahoo, sailfish on the reef edge, bottom fishing wrecks, and anchored on patch reef or reef edges. Since the patch reef and reef edge fishing is unique to the Keys, it is worth pondering for a bit.

Overall, it's pretty easy: anchor with boat over depth of choice, couple of blocks of frozen chum over the side in chum bag, and live bait or frozen shrimp, cut bait or ballyhoo chunks in the slick. Generally spinning rods, fairly light line, light hooks, drifted back

Yellowtails, ceros, king, and spadefish

into the slick. Not complicated—at least not to explain. But what happens is where the fun begins; and you never know what to expect.

You hope for yellowtails, those tasty little guys from one to five or six pounds; they fight hard and are a delicacy on the table. But often the slick will load up with blue runners, yellow jacks or jack crevalle. Maybe ladyfish to jump all across the surface, always a cobia or two (usually 12 to 15 lb., but one four day run had 35-pounders or better every day).

And then there are the various "toothy guys": cero mackerel, Spanish mackerel, and king mackerel. Once in the slick, a wire trace is required. Often a grouper—red, black, or gag—will come up from the bottom and try to rip the rod out of your hands! Or an amberjack.

Mangroves, mutton, and grouper

And then, with luck, the mangrove snappers or mutton snappers will join the party; and sometimes, if the bait is big enough, a cubera snapper with huge teeth (lobsters are their food of choice, hence teethies) will show. On any given day, all in the same slick. Not to mention the occasional school of spadefish, a sea trout or two, porgies, redfish, lane snappers, and so on. Often a fish will show that requires a sneak peek into the book. By the way, the squirrel fish above? Also called a wench. Go figure!

And just to spice up the day, there will always be a sharkie or two coming by, generally followed by hooking one or two or three remoras—each up to three-feet long with huge suction cup heads. If a school of live ballyhoo show (and generally they do), a Sabiki rig or Ballyhoop will fill the live well, and more fun yet!

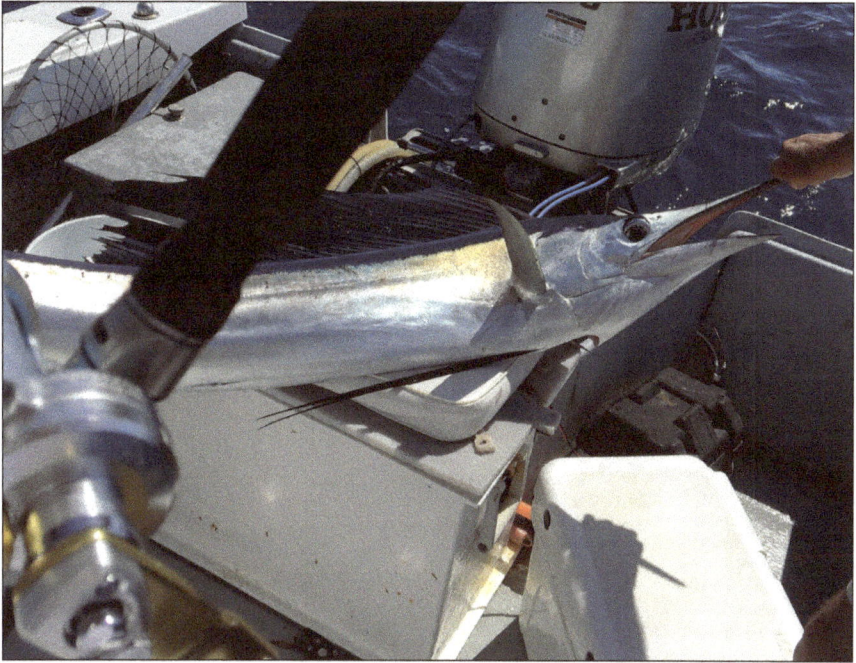

Sailfish

Cast a live 'hoo away from the boat and hang on; most often a smoker king or big cero will crash it and give a 10-to-20-minute fight. Or a cobia or a wahoo or a sailfish.

Yep, this is way different fishing. Lotsa fun to be sure, often great table fare, and generally no more than a 20-minute run.

Chapter 11:
Love Tile Fishing

⚓

You have likely figured out by now that I really like tilefish. Why? Well, three important reasons: 1) best tasting fish in the ocean, like big thick chunks of fresh sweet lobster; 2) once you find a "covey" of them, they're very aggressive and fight like hell; and 3) best tasting fish in the ocean (worth saying twice!). Lotsa offshore folks think of tiles as backup to the normal tuna, mahi, billfish—sorta like the French fries but not the steak. Me, just the opposite. Often, I either head out specifically for tiles or give trolling a couple of hours, maybe put a couple of tuna in the box, then drop for tiles.

Tiles come in two distinct and different species under the same genus. Golden tiles are generally found burrowed deep on mud bottoms, down 600 to 900 feet. They get big, running up to 60 or so lb., golden color with blue tinge, and hunk of flesh on top of the head. A beautiful fish. Bluelines are a bit smaller, run to 22 to 23 lb., found in 350 to 500 feet on rocky structure bottom. Also a pretty fish, silvery blue with distinct blue line running from gill to eye socket. Both taste great and both fight like hell!

My strong preference is the blueline for several reasons: they tend to be more of a schooling fish, are very predatory, and are far stronger than their size would indicate. Once we find them, if the current is not ridiculously strong, I put my anglers on jigging rods with 30-lb. braid, 850-gram jigs, and high-speed Tallica reels. And it is a blast! Often the jig barely gets to bottom before it's slammed and the fight begins. Luckily, we've found several areas where the fish tend to average 15-plus lb. so a limit is a great day for the table.

Mid-July 2020, forecast for next day 2 feet, 10 seconds, light and variable. Dave Long, captain of private rig *ForTUNAte* wanted a tile trip and Dr. Pat had the next day off and wanted to bring son James, so we had a plan. We took my rig, planned to leave the dock a bit early at 9:30 a.m. One of the interesting bits about tiles, they tend to bite best when the sun is at its highest; no clue as to why, just the way it is. The four of us pulled off on time; one electric for prospecting if needed and four jigging rigs. One set of numbers I have labeled "Fish Market": it's damn near a lock cinch. We only hit it once a season, but it's damned good great really.

Got to the numbers at 11:15 a.m., 63.3 miles, flat calm. Got the jig rigs ready to go; five-foot leaders of 200-lb. mono, one leader for jig rigged with three 12/0 heavy duty circles—gonna be fun! First drop with electric proved we were there; soon as we hit bottom, rod tip went off, flicked the switch and brought up our first two tiles. Not big, maybe 10 to 12 pounds each, but they were there! Slow, easy current, cobalt blue water, 397 feet, and lotsa fish. I took the helm, we stowed the electric and did the drift again; three jigs down, three hooked up. Dave was great,

Doc with four tiles hooked—they're winning!

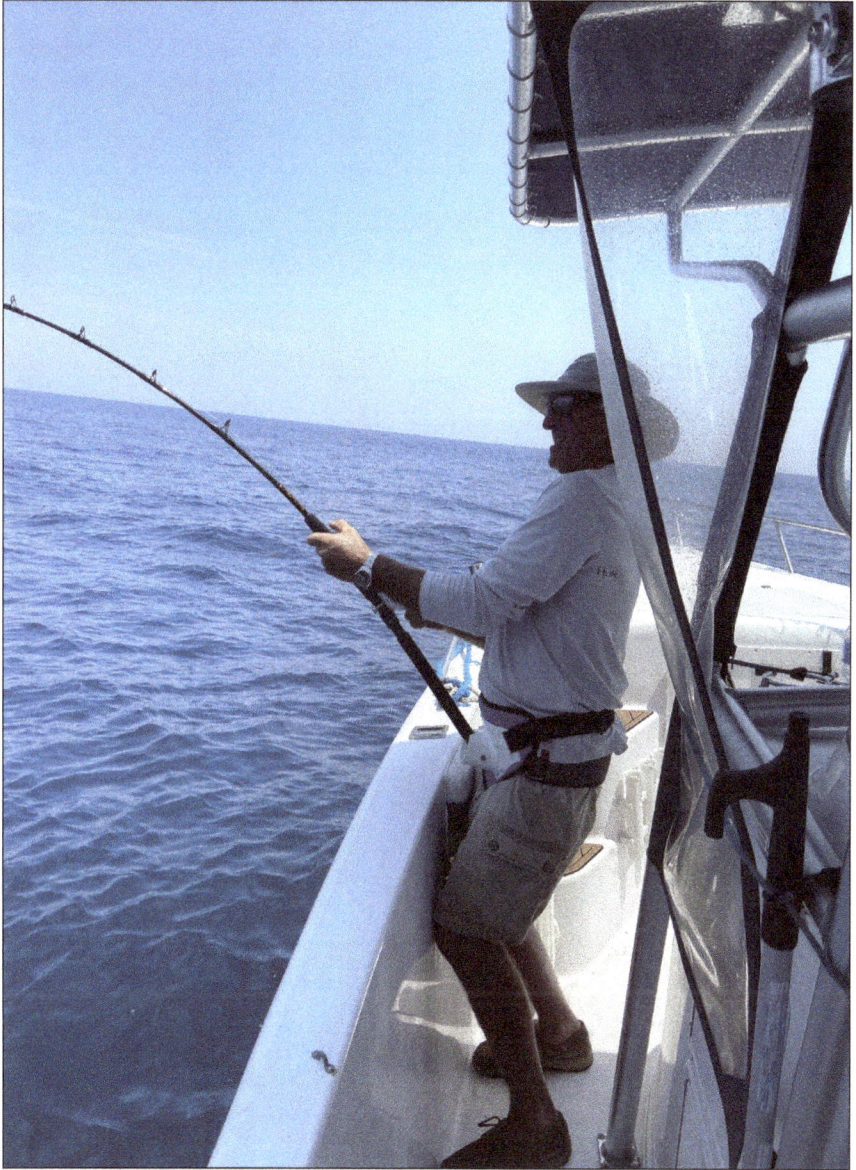

He's got them under control

One of four on same rod

gaffing, unhooking, stowing fish. Each drift more of the same; Doc, James, and Dave were having a blast.

Set another drift with one difference—Doc had the three-hook leader, we baited with cobia belly, and he dropped. Bam! One fish, then two, then a third—and then a fourth! Yep, Doc had four tiles hooked on a fairly light (20-lb. class) rod with a two-speed Tallica 12 reel; damn that was fun to watch. (Check out the picture: he's almost on his knees before he got them under control). After twenty minutes, from 400-feet down, four fish on the deck; biggest one 20 lb., three others maybe 10 lb. each. Great fun!

Two hours, limited out, fish boxes full—202 pounds on the hoof. And still flat calm, high sun, warm and beautiful. We picked up at 2:35 p.m., tied up at the fish cleaner less than two hours later. Doc and James slept on bean bags, while Dave and I solved the worlds remaining problems, heading for the barn at 37 knots while sitting with our feet up, and an ice-cold soda in hand. Blessed! A day's fishing just doesn't get any better.

CHAPTER 12:
SEQUEL TO "WHERE WE AT, HOSS?"

⚓

If you remember the story in my first book, our "captain" for the day ran out of fuel and the Coast Guard towed us in with a topless young girl dancing on the bow. With that picture in mind, we fished the next day. Our anglers were two guys, both new to offshore, both friends from work (a multi-national office equipment company). Both had been at the dock the day before when we arrived in full glory! And both were with their wives who, to say the least, were completely bewildered by the unfolding scene. The wives were different as night and day. The wife of the sales guy was happy, friendly, funny, and seemed to enjoy the spectacle. The wife of the sales manager—not so much.

In fact, she didn't seem to like the whole deal: fishing, crowded dock, boats, etc.—no, not at all. She was tall, very pretty, but a bit of the "holier than thou" persuasion. She wore outfits straight out of the Talbots catalog, too much jewelry, matching sandals, etc.—clearly a "tight ass". On the day in question, she was wearing a floral dress, buttons all the way up, with matching belt and visor ... clearly not the outfit of choice for meeting your husband's boat coming in from offshore; his first trip offshore no less. She was there not only to see, but to be seen.

As we started to back into our slip, the usual crowd gathered to see and comment on the days catch. I was on the helm, she was in the group standing when, all of a sudden, she screams out, "I can do it, too!" She unbuttons the top of her dress, pulls down her bra, and starts flailing her breasts wildly. We were sorta speechless as she did her best to show her stuff to everyone, in every direction. After a few minutes, folks quickly dispersed, and she quieted down, and her husband said quietly, "you can put them away now."

We cleaned the boat, never said a word about it, had the fish cleaned, then went to dinner. It would be fair to say their relationship was "strained" that evening. He declined to fish the next day, and they left early with a short note left on the table. Their divorce was final within a year.

Chapter 13:
The Father of the Mate ...
One of the Best Lines Ever!

⚓

June 2010, Indian River. Had a young guy as part-time mate, we traded fishing trips for his education. He worked hard, knew enough, and was desperate to learn more a fun young guy. We fun-fished mostly, inshore stuff, flounder and sea bass generally. We took various friends, friends of friends, even folks we met at the Dockside Bar; we had fun. On occasion, my mate would show up with one or more young ladies—some he'd just met—but always a kick, usually sending them home with fresh fish dinner.

On the day noted above, the mate called and asked if we could take his Dad. Of course, we could, and off we went. The plan was easy, our norm—head out to the Coral Beds for flounder. Sea was calm, half dozen keepers in the box, and lotsa radio chatter of bluefins near the 30 line. Only about ten miles to the 12 Fathom Lump then five more miles to the 30. Mate and I looked at each for a few, and then he said, "My Dad has never caught a big fish. Whaddya think?" We carry a complement of offshore tackle, just in case, so we decided to give it a go. Flounder tackle in, two 30s and two 50s out and rigged.

We put out at the Lump and trolled off to the 30 line; lotsa boats and chatter, but fishing was slow. Fifties on the riggers, 30 on one flat and a second 30 set way back. And, after two hours we were bit—solid tuna hookup on the way back. (Note: we set the 30 as the way back intentionally, the fish were schoolies and figured better fight on lighter rig). Typical tuna fight, nothing unusual, couple good runs (didn't help with boat), circles at the end, mate gaffed the fish, school bluefin maybe 50-ish lb. But, pretty long fight, maybe 15 to 20 minutes, mate swung fish over the gunwale, his Dad looked at the mate and at me and then uttered the best line yet: "Holy hell, what happened to rest of him?"

Perfect line to sum up a new guy on a tuna rod! We stowed the tackle, had bunch of great laughs, cracked a cold one, and bogeyed to the barn. It was a good, fun day!

Chapter 14:
Icy Straits

⚓

It all began a year after retiring. Having traveled constantly for business (often taking flights to and from work on Mondays and Thursdays) we hadn't traveled much for vacations. But my wife was anxious to travel, so once retired we agreed to travel five or six weeks each year. Our first year's travel included a cruise on a small boat (120 foot with 10 cabins) through parts of Alaska, primarily the Inside Passage.

And so, given the smallish ship and somewhat personal service, a few weeks before the trip the operators called my wife to inquire if we had special interests for food and drink and activities. Eileen had a long discussion and noted that I liked to fish. They promised fishing tackle would be aboard and that there would be opportunities to fish each evening as the boat anchored for the night. Having no clue as to where or what, it sounded good to me.

Well, there was fishing tackle aboard ... sorta! Three conventional outfits, each with terminal tackle (maybe 9/0 hook, heavy short leader, each with a three-pound lead ball weight) leaning up against the rear bulkhead, after which was a six-foot deck extension with several chairs. Fishing tackle, to be sure, but it did leave a bit to be desired. Probably not a problem though since my expectations were minimal.

First night anchoring out in 500-foot depth, decided not to think about it. Night two, though, we set anchor early in 300 foot so decided to give it a try, at which point I realized there was no thought of bait. Anywhere! So, after heading to the galley and searching through the refrigerator, it seemed as if the best bet would be two strips of bacon, set to flutter in the current. Worth a try. By this time, a handful of folks had joined me on the back deck (it was cocktail hour) and seemed to enjoy the spectacle of a guy using crappy tackle fishing the bottom in 300-foot wa-ter—with bacon strips. And, truth be told, it was a grin. Catching expectations ... none! So, ordered a Grey Goose on the rocks with a twist and sat down to enjoy the evening, soaking bacon strips to everyone's amusement.

After maybe an hour, figured time to check the bait, got two turns on the reel handle and got slammed; hooked up! And to a solid fish! The group went silent and after several short powerful runs, up came a halibut of 40-ish pounds. While trying to figure how to boat it (no net and no gaff), the chef comes running out with a hand gaff of sorts, kneels down and boats my first ever halibut to cheers and raised glasses. Immediately the chef asks if he can serve it for dinner (of course!) and I bask in the light of success. Not one to risk possibly being skunked, that ended the evening's fishing.

The next two nights anchor sets were in way deep water so just relaxed (while continuing to enjoy my kudos). And then in

Glacier Bay, the boat burned up several injectors on their 12v71s and had to wait for parts to be flown in. We had a free, unplanned day, and the trip operator asked if we had special interests, so of course, I asked if there were charter boats available. To my surprise there were, and a trip was booked for me out of Icy Straits—on a 25-foot aluminum charter. Two other passengers wanted to go also, so off we went.

Fast forward to the dock, complete with 25-foot ladder to allow for huge tidal swings. We clamber onto the boat (maybe 45 degrees, windy and overcast) and head out. The captain was clearly knowledgeable and ran maybe 10 miles to drop on several pinnacles at 500 feet surrounded by 700- to 800-foot depths. He baited the other two folks with 4 lb. leads and 6- to 8-inch cut baits, then asked if I was willing to try for bigger fish at the risk of no bites. The hook rig was maybe 4 feet of green parachute cord with two 12/0 hooks set up maybe 12 inches apart. The bait was a whole filet cut from maybe 5 to 6 lb. salmon, double hooked and dropped to the bottom. Each of the other fishermen caught a halibut—one was his second—when my rod suddenly bowed deep and line began to scream off the Tyrnos 30! Hooked up to a very heavy fish and the fight was on. And then, after maybe 15 or 20 minutes, the captain began throwing cherry bombs, maybe every 10 minutes or so, to keep the sea lions away from the fish. It was a strong, heavy fish, and took a long time to gain line. Finally, began getting a few turns on him and after two hours, we had a monster halibut at boat side!

Next surprise: Captain takes out a short barreled .410 shotgun and fires three slugs into the fish's head. And in minutes, it's over, the fish is dead weight and we all struggle to boat it. It measure

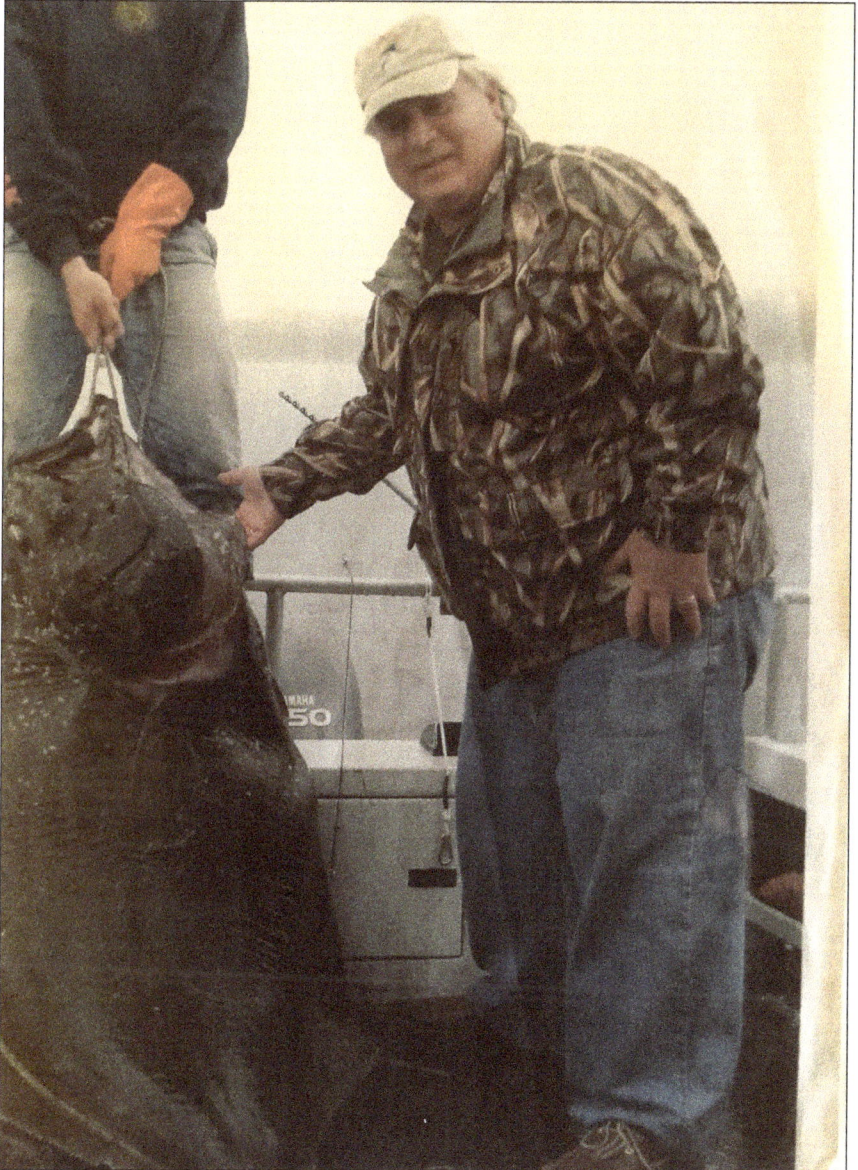

Author with 80-inch, 244-lb. halibut caught at 500-foot depth
in Icy Straights, Alaska

6-foot 5-inches length and approximately 24 inches in depth. It's my second halibut and it's a monster! We're done; three small fish maybe 30 to 35 lb. and the big one. As we get to the dock, the processor is waiting and we split the fish three ways, each giving our requested cuts and delivery address, and return to our now fixed boat. Turns out the "big one" weighed 244 lb. and was 80 inches in length.

My wife's trip turned out to be a wonderful cruise for her and great fishing trip for me. To this day, the folks on our cruise probably think of me as a good halibut fisherman. I shall never spoil it by telling them I've only ever caught two.

The big one, after being gutted, weighed in at 244 lbs.; we three each got roughly 60 lbs. of great eating. I was told, but have no way to verify, that our halibut was the largest taken that year in the Inside Passage. Even a blind squirrel ....

CHAPTER 15:
JUST A BIG BULLY!

⚓

When fishing the Lower Keys (from the Seven Mile Bridge to Key West) there are multiple ways to fish: back country, Gulf, deep drop, trolling, patch reefs, reef edge, and more. Probably the most popular by far is to run the 8 to 10 miles to the reef edge, anchor and set out a bag of chum. And after 20 or 30 minutes a variety of fish will moved into the slick, and drifting a cut bait, live shrimp, or live pilchard creates pretty steady action. It's not unusual to catch 10 to 15 species in the same day, often one than another: blackfin tuna, bonito (boneheads here), king and cero and Spanish mackerel, spadefish, yellowtails and mangrove snappers, blue runners, groupers, amberjacks. Typical tackle used is light to medium spinners, 20 lb. main line with fluoro leaders.

And, as one would suspect, the combination of chum slick and fish being caught often attracts other unwanted "visitors," hence, it's not unusual for a fish or two to be donated to a Sharkie! It's generally a pretty common occurrence: Sharkie takes a fish or two, nobody minds terribly, and everyone goes back to bringing

Lemon shark 8-10', hooked and released
after helping himself to our catch for a bit.

Good day on king mackerel - smoker and fish dip -
Lower Keys specialties.

in the catch. Occasionally a shark will become a nuisance and, if so, somebody will pick up a conventional outfit, hook, and fight the shark until release; shark goes away, things back to normal.

And, so, on Tuesday, while catching yellowtails, a good-sized lemon shark helped himself to a fish now and again. After a while, he did get a bit overzealous, so we hooked and fought him for maybe 15 minutes, got him up beside the boat and released him; he left us quickly thereafter. Pretty much the way it's supposed to go.

But, on Thursday, same general area, catching the normal variety of fish, an unusually large bonito hit and just before getting him to the boat a large (as in very large) bull shark came out if nowhere and crashed the bonito! He hit it with such violent force that we stood open mouthed. He was every bit of 12 foot, perhaps longer, and maybe 4 foot in width. His pectoral fins looked like wings on a small plane. He was a monster! Stunningly beautiful in his own way.

And then, to our surprise, he decided to take up residence under our boat! He didn't seem to bother the smaller fish yellowtails and the like but every time we hooked anything large enough to pull drag or fight for more than a few minutes, here comes Big Bully! Once we realized the rules of his game, we pulled anchor and ran maybe a mile and set up again. Chum bag over, wait for a while, start to fish.

A mile away, an hour later, bonito hooked, and (big surprise), our buddy is back. But this time even more aggressive and more violent! He seemed to realize that he was in control (he was!) and now he charged everything we hooked. He was way too big to try to hook and release; he was clearly focused on our boat and

Smoker King
45 lbs.

showed no intention of leaving for greener pastures. He often hit the boat with his tail, throwing water in his wake. He clearly preferred his meal to be tired and easy pickings.

So, we thought about it (not too long, though), decided we were getting low on chum, almost out of shrimp, and clearly not going to add much to the fish box. Thus, we did what made the most sense we pulled anchor and headed for the barn. Once everything put up, boat cleaned, we drank a cold beer to the Big Bully!

CHAPTER 16:
WORLD'S BEST FISH'N' LOCATION?
AN OPINION ...

⚓

Depending on age and circumstances, we have all fished lotsa places. Most of us have fished many of the East Coast spots, some have fished the Bahamas, the West Coast, Costa Rica, Australia, Hawaii and the myriad of places of lesser renown: Cape Verde, Chatham, Canada, and others. Each has its supporters, and each has its own "special feel," its own vibe. At their best, each is grand and glorious in its own way!

But, when you start to consider the tougher questions, oftentimes the specifics begin to falter. Questions such as quality and availability of boats and crews, quality of tackle, accommodations, accessibility, and the clincher fishable seasons. Given these and other questions, when we sort through the world's best fishing locations, not many hold up. Sure, the argument will be made, this or that place in this or that season and the answer will hold water. So likely we each ask the questions and come up with our own answer. Here is mine.

Without doubt and without question, in my humble opinion,

Oregon Inlet on the North Carolina coast is far and away the best fishing overall, maybe on the planet! Here is why:

1. Best boats, best captains, and best crews on average anywhere in the world.

2. Proximity to world class fishing spots: The Point, the Tower, the Cigar, the Tuna Hole, the 800 Line, and on and on. Generally, not further than 30 to 45 miles, some a bit further, but all in or close to the Gulf Stream. And all hold fish.

3. Billfish from April through November, blue and white marlin, sailfish, spearfish and daytime swordfish. They are all there: grand slams are not unusual.

4. Tuna available pretty much year-round, limits of yellowfins frequent, wintertime giant bluefins abound, big eyes and blackfins they are all there.

5. Dolphin (or mahi or dorado) are thicker and more abundant than anywhere else known.

6. And the seasonal runs of cobia, king mackerel, tilefish, groupers, and so on all there.

7. And the fish and fishing are there year-round.

World class accommodations, easy access by car or air. Top notch, but there's more MUCH MORE!

Oregon Inlet is the home of the Carolina Flare, the finest custom-built sportfishing boats in the world. Boats built not by factories but by hand by men who ran charter boats for years, crossing "the bar" twice daily in most any weather, learning what works and what does not as they worked the sea. Boats built by men like Paul Spencer (Spencer Yachts), John Bayliss, Ricky Scarborough, Paul Mann, Buddy Davis, Omie Tillett, and others like them. They learned the basics from Warren O'Neal, then overlaid what they had learned as they built the best sea boats to be found anywhere.

And then, add the working charter captains of today: Bull Tolson, Brynner Parks, Dickie Harris, Sam Stokes, and all the guys at the Oregon Inlet Fishing Center and at Pirates Cove; they not only compete, but they share information and more importantly they look after each other and take pride in the fleet success. They are the backbone of the world-class fleet.

And so, the magic is real combine the best boats, the best captains, the best fishing with easy access, proximity to great accommodations, a short run to the fish and you have, in my humble opinion, the BEST in the world!

(Disclaimer: I admit to possibly not being objective, having learned offshore fishing at OI and having owned Buddy Davis Hull #1 as a charter boat. But I have fished most of the top spots in the world, and my opinion holds).

Chapter 17:
The WMO, the Dolphin, the Sinking, the Opossum, and the Late-Night News!

⚓

It all ties together, read on!

January 2007, my wife and I plan a mid-summer driving trip to the Canadian Maritimes a slow ten-day drive to relax and just get away. April 2007, my buddies decide to give the White Marlin Open one last shot: run the *Fight-N-Lady* up from Oregon Inlet (Joe's boat, Sam Stokes captain), dock at Big John Evans' slip at Harbour Island, two mates.

At dinner with wives, the boys mention the Open. I guess I looked forlorn because Eileen says, "Oh, go fishing, I'll fly out to California and visit my friend." And now, I am part of the crew: six of us as anglers, captain, and two mates. We were ready!

August 2007, everything set: fueled up, iced down, tackle, baits and best of all three day forecast of calm seas. We plan to fish our 3 days of 5 on Monday, Tuesday, and Wednesday. Good to go.

Monday, run to Poor Mans, set up in 50 fathoms and begin to troll; long riggers, short riggers, flat lines and shotgun all looked good. And we did well. If memory serves, we caught a few yellowfins, went 3 of 5 on whites. Joe did have a white that came oh so close but missed length by an inch. Good start!

Tuesday, tried a bit further north, put out in forty and worked to the Hundred line. Just as we crossed over the edge, the shotgun went off. Chris Evans was up and after a twenty-minute fight, landed a huge bull dolphin weighing in officially at 54 lb. And in first place in the dolphin category.

Wednesday, still flat calm; decided to head for the Baltimore Canyon, ready to set out by 8:00 a.m. But sun not fully up, and maybe 10 miles from the Canyon, Capt. Sam gets a call from Mike Bennett he's in trouble. Mike was a mate for Sam for years, a good friend and currently captain of a private boat, a 65 foot custom built in NC. Quick discussion and we change course and head to Mike. We get there and his boat is sinking they hit a deadhead (floating end of sunken piling) at speed—and cockpit is half full of water. We transfer as much as we can to our boat and get five of seven folks aboard. Another Carolina boat picks up two and the boat sinks until just the bow sticks out of the water, held there by an air pocket. Coast Guard asks us to stand by and release the other Carolina boat to fish. We stand by with the five passengers and wait. Coast Guard C-130 circles to assess and at about 2:30 a CG boat arrives and releases us. We return to Ocean City and are told by the Tournament that we did not use up a fishing day and still had our one day left.

Thursday, wind up, seas rough, we stay put. It's a lay day for us; clean up a bit, rig tackle, go to lunch and relax. Watching a boat in trouble is not an easy time and we welcomed the break. The boys either sleep in the boat or in John's townhouse. It's restful, nice, and needed.

Friday, more wind lots more and forecast 4- to 5-foot seas. But it's our last day, so the boys decide to go. But yours truly (me, the author) qualifies as a rough weather wimp, so as we ready to pull off, I bail and tell the boys to do well and will see them when they get in. Back to Bethany for the day, glad to be on land and spend day not getting tossed around. And get a call from Eileen: we are invited to neighborhood monthly dinner at 7:00 p.m., she has accepted, and we are going. She expects to make it home in time for quick shower, change of clothes, and expects me to be ready. About 4:00-ish, head to the dock to meet the boys. Rough day, no qualifying fish, everything covered in salt; glad to not be there!

So, after we find out that Chris' dolphin has won the category, helping clean up and racing home to shower and change, I have no time to spare. Expecting Eileen about 6:45 then leave by 7:00-ish for dinner. (Man plans, God laughs!). Jump in shower, clean up, and still wet, head to bedroom to dry off and dress.

Our bedroom door has a master closet long and wide with two sliding doors. I slide the left one open and look for a shirt while drying off. I pull open two shirts to consider, and the shirts get pulled back! What? This cannot be. So, I try again same result so I close the door and ponder. This time, towel set aside, still in my birthday suit, I pull open the shirts: and hanging there on the clothes rod is a very large, big teeth visible, unhappy opossum!

Mystery solved, sorta, but what to do? Eileen due home momentarily, unhappy opossum in our closet, me and a towel and the critter staring at each other. What next?

Thinking quickly, I realized a fish net is in the storage room, so I close the door, get the net and return. Open the closet, grab the critter gently using the towel to hold him so I don't hurt him, manage to get him into the net (he's not at all happy, hissing loudly and clacking his needle teeth) holding him down with the towel, he and I head for the backyard. I release him and he waddles off quickly. And as I walk into the house, Eileen comes in from the front, me in birthday suit carrying a net and a towel. She gives a look, shakes her head, and says, "I don't wanna know". She wears the outfit she has on, I pour her a glass of wine, dress quickly and we go to dinner, with me having no clues as to how NOT to tell her about the opossum in the closet which would surely be scary.

Home from dinner, only discussed fishing and California. Ready to relax, Eileen opens closet door, pulls back, looks at me and says, "What is that smell?" Well, now totally busted, and realizing there are opossum droppings covering the closet floor, I have to tell the story. And, to my surprise, she understands and fills in the blank!

Unbeknownst to me, given that I was out of town for four days fishing, Eileen had called the plumber to fix a leak in the bathtub, which abuts the back of the closet. Plumber had to remove tiles and repair under the tub with plywood and left it open overnight to dry out. Came the next day to finish the job and close it in which he did. But our furry friend found a nice place to hang out (pun intended) and got closed in as he dozed through the day!

Mystery solved, wife not scared, won a tournament category; all good!

But here's the kicker: while in California with her girlfriend, they saw a newscast with a short clip about a disabled boat off the Maryland coast being tended to by another boat, taken by the CG in the C-130. To which Eileen said to Susan, "I think that may be the boat Jeff and the boys are on!" They laughed, said probably not, and had another glass of Prosecco!

Go figure!

Chapter 18:
Right Fish, Wrong Canyon

⚓

September 2016 perfect next day forecast for offshore run; a neighbor surf fishing guy wants to go and my buddy who runs a local headboat has the day off, it's a plan. We meet at my boat for quick run for a shot at tuna and mahi, pull off dock at 10:00 a.m. with the sea flat and calm. I'm on the helm, neighbor Ron in bolster beside me, Roger in cockpit rigging up four 30s and a 50 for way back line. We set for Baltimore Canyon tip, running 38 knots. About ten minutes out, I lazily click on the waypoint, but more keeping an eye on neighbor who has never been out sight of land. (Emphasis on the lazy here.) The run should be about an hour and forty minutes to set out.

The day is glorious, boat running fine, neighbor enthralled, and the cockpit set up. But something is just not right; we should be almost there, yet we are not yet in forty fathoms. I decide to actually look, and to my embarrassment, I clicked on the wrong waypoint and we are heading slightly north of the Baltimore, toward the south tip of the Wilmington Canyon! Ron has no idea of course, but Roger just laughs, and we continue on to the

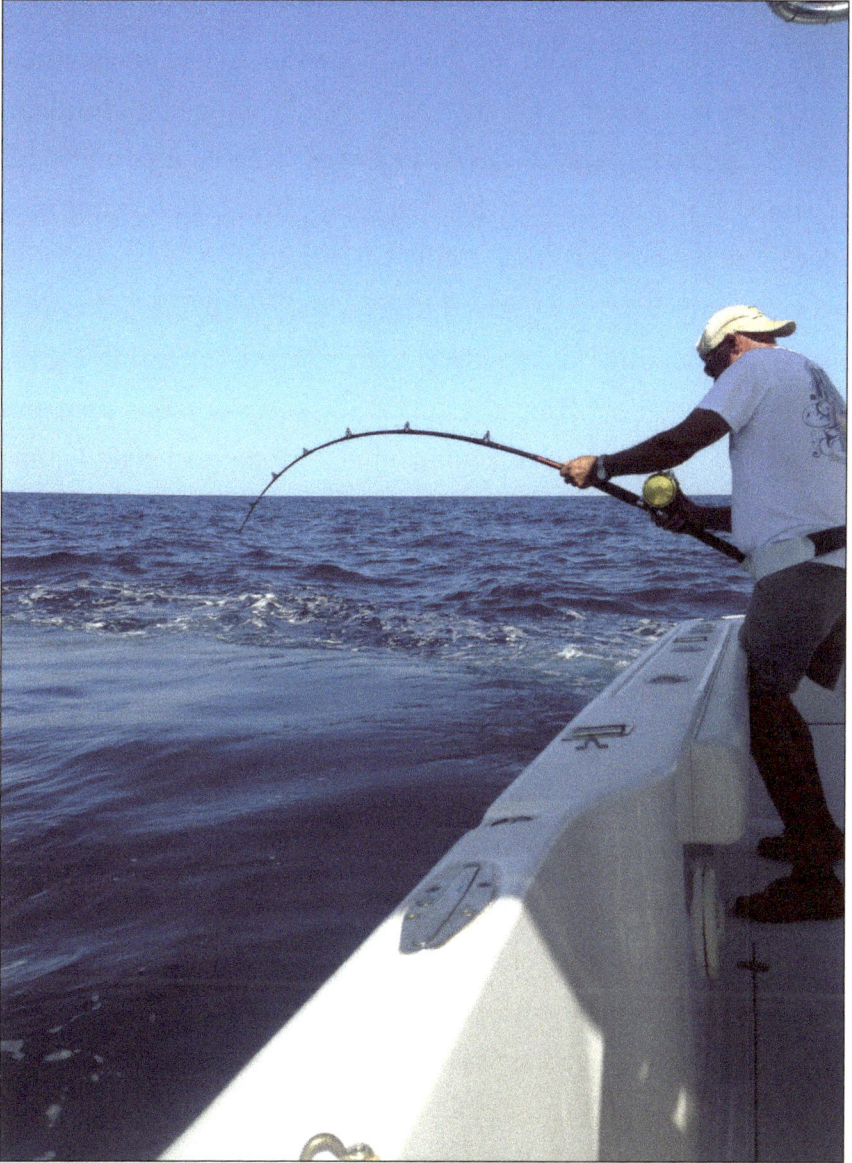

Blue one giving Roger a workout on standup 30.
At this point, fish still winning!

wrong canyon.

Grass everywhere from forty fathoms to overboard as far as you can see. Nonetheless, we set up our spread and while pulling grass, constantly manage to put two gaffers in the boat. Frustrated, we pick up and run ten miles south along the Hundred, and the grass lessens up and it becomes fishable although still scattered grass, and looks fishy: fliers, deep blue cobalt water, nice edge. We set out, left long and left flat out, right long goes out, we're in heavy scattered grass, the pin pops, I think it's grass when all of a sudden, the 30 drag begins to sound like tearing canvas we're hooked up! A Blue one jumps 300 yards out, so I turn and run parallel with him and bend in a bit so Roger can pick up line. After ten or fifteen frantic minutes, we get the other two lines cleared and stowed and settle into the fight.

My angler Roger is a pro and knows what to do and when to do it, the boat handles easily and seas calm, shifting into our favor. Ron, meanwhile, simply looks at me and says, "I didn't know fish really got that big. Honest, I didn't." He enjoyed every second!

We worked the fish on a light drag, 10 lb. on a 30 standup; Roger in the cockpit and yours truly on the helm, everything went as it should. We kept the fish within maybe 100 yards and wore her out enough to get a release while she was still strong. The fight lasted maybe an hour and a half. We called the fish 325-350, average blue marlin for Mid-Atlantic late season, but a trophy on standup 30, especially on a fun run trip!

By now, it was 4:00 p.m., two gaffer mahi in the box, and a release, so we picked up for the barn. At just before six, we tied up at Hookem for fish cleaning, and where the headboat that Roger runs is docked. Bert, the owner, came out to ask how we did. Roger, being pleased with the day said, "Well, we left at 10:00 a.m., boated two gaffers, released a Blue and tied up at six." Bert, who sees everything at the Marina, looked straight at him and said, "Not so!" Roger looked bit bewildered until Bert smirked and said, "You guys didn't pull out until 10:15."

Some days things go right even they go wrong! Right fish, wrong canyon.

Author, Joe Perez, and Dave Mutz with 361-lb. swordfish

Author in 1963 with stringer of trout in New Jersey

ABOUT THE AUTHOR

⚓

Waxman likes fishing, bit of hunting and more fishing ... on his boat or with marina friends. He can be found from May till December in Bethany Beach, Delaware; boat below docked at Indian River North Shore. He is either fishing, sitting at the bar at Hammerheads Dockside, or hanging around the marina. From December till early May in Cudjoe Key, Florida ... also either fishing or hanging around at Kiki's on Little Torch. Boat in the Keys is smaller 24-foot Grady White; you don't need much boat for short runs in calm seas.

Jeff can be reached on email at Jeffwaxman1@gmail.com. Only positive comments accepted.

Author's 35 ZFC Center Console